P9-CDU-478

THE STORY OF THE
HOLOCAUST

Clive A. Lawton

W

FRANKLIN WATTS
A Division of Grolier Publishing
NEW YORK • LONDON • HONG KONG • SYDNEY
DANBURY, CONNECTICUT

About the Author

Clive A. Lawton is an educator, broadcaster, and writer. A former headteacher, he has been involved in the development of Holocaust studies, and is vice-chairman of the Anne Frank Educational Trust, UK.

The author and publishers would like to thank the Holocaust Educational Trust for their help in preparing this book.

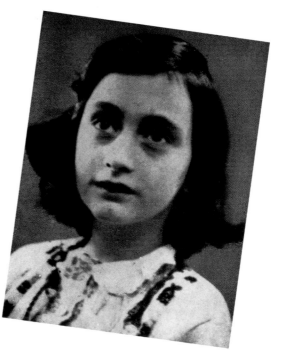

Library of Congress Cataloging-in-Publication Data

Lawton, Clive
    The story of the Holocaust/Clive A. Lawton
      p. cm.
    Includes bibliographical references and index.

    Summary: Examines the events of the Holocaust within the context of World War II and Germany's economic and political history, while highlighting the main figures of the time.

    ISBN 0-531-14524-7 (lib.bdg)
    ISBN 0-531-15376-2 (pbk)
    1. Holocaust. Jewish (1939–1945) Juvenile literature. [1. Holocaust, Jewish (1939–1945) 2. Germany—Politics and government–1933–1945.] I. Title.
    D804.34.L38 2000
    940.53'18–dc21
             99–29047
             CIP

First published in 1999 by Franklin Watts

First American edition 1999 by Franklin Watts
A Division of Grolier Publishing
90 Sherman Turnpike
Danbury, CT 06816

Visit Franklin Watts on the Internet at:
http://publishing.grolier.com

© Franklin Watts 1999

Printed in Hong Kong.

CONTENTS

HOW COULD THIS HAPPEN?

Europe in the 1930s was beginning to look like the world we are used to today. Television was introduced, medicine was rapidly improving, and telephones, radio, and cinema newsreels let people know what was happening around the world, almost as it happened.

In Central Europe, countries like Germany and Austria were culturally very exciting. Music, art, literature, architecture, sociology, and psychology were all developing quickly. Many people were confident that the world was becoming more "civilized".

But there were also many poor people in Germany and Austria who felt increasingly angry. In 1933, Germany followed Italy's example and elected Fascist leaders with strong ideas about what needed to be done.

In Germany, the people voted for the National Socialist Party, called the Nazi Party for short. The Nazis ruled through teaching hatred, stirring up envy, and encouraging fear. Their central idea was that everyone was *not* equal, but that some groups of people were "superior" and others "inferior." The Nazis also believed that certain groups, especially Jews, were not just at the bottom of the heap of humanity, but that they were actually dangerous and should be destroyed.

In the pages that follow, we will trace how these ideas led to the most systematic massacre the world has ever seen. Over 10 million people, including 6 million Jews, were killed by the Nazis in what is now known as the Holocaust. And it all happened in a place and in a time not so very different from our own.

Bergen-Belsen, 1945. A pit full of bodies discovered at the Bergen-Belsen concentration camp at the end of the Second World War. Who were they, and how did they get there?

THE JEWS IN EUROPE

Since Roman times, there have been Jews all across Europe. Many Jews were successful in the countries in which they had settled. But they were also often subject to anti-Jewish feeling—known as anti-Semitism—from the Christians around them.

In the Middle Ages, Church leaders taught that the Jews were responsible for the death of Christ, and were therefore evil. As a result, many Jewish communities suffered oppression, discrimination, expulsion, and massacre. By the 19th century, the Christian Church had more moderate views, but by this time the habit of persecuting Jews was deeply ingrained. People in the 19th century turned to science and began to create false scientific theories to support their anti-Semitism.

▲ **The Crusades, c.1150.** Christian armies, on a "holy" crusade to liberate Jerusalem from the Saracens in the 12th century, stopped to attack any Jews they found on the way.

▶ **Shopwindows smashed in Wales, 1922.** Hatred and mistrust of Jews was common throughout Europe in the 19th and early 20th centuries. When life became hard for the miners in South Wales in 1922, the miners attacked Jewish-owned shops.

By the beginning of the 20th century, Jews were at the forefront of arts, science, medicine, and industrial development in many countries. At one level, Jews had fit into Western society and were fully integrated into social, commercial, and artistic life. But the idea of a multicultural society had not yet arrived. In many European countries, Jews were still the only sizeable minority, and remained the focus of racist feeling that sometimes flared into violence.

The Frank family. By the 1930s, many Western Jews, such as the Franks, were successful and prosperous. By 1945, the whole Frank family, except the father, was dead. (Anne Frank is third from the right.)

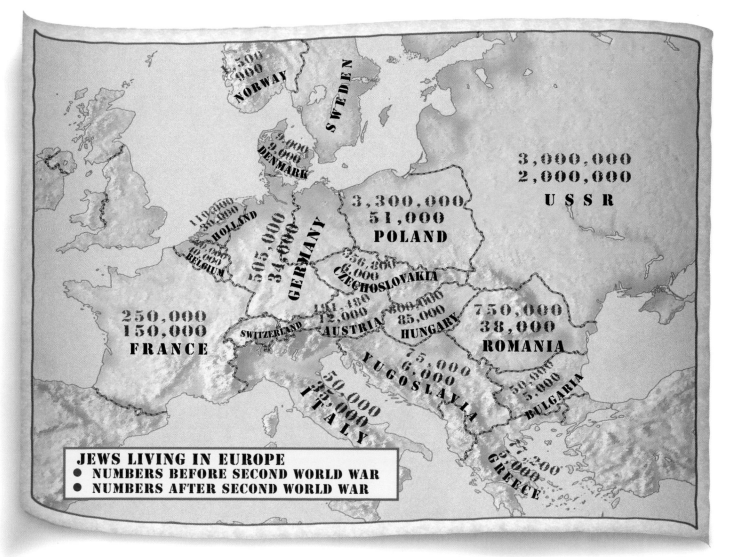

1,500,000
NORWAY

SWEDEN

9,000
9,000
DENMARK

110,000
30,000
HOLLAND

40,000
40,000
BELGIUM

505,000
34,000
GERMANY

3,300,000
51,000
POLAND

3,000,000
2,000,000
USSR

356,800
6,000
CZECHOSLOVAKIA

191,480
12,000
AUSTRIA

800,000
85,000
HUNGARY

750,000
38,000
ROMANIA

250,000
150,000
FRANCE

SWITZERLAND

75,000
6,000
YUGOSLAVIA

50,000
5,000
BULGARIA

50,000
35,000
ITALY

77,200
2,000
GREECE

JEWS LIVING IN EUROPE
- **NUMBERS BEFORE SECOND WORLD WAR**
- **NUMBERS AFTER SECOND WORLD WAR**

THE DEPRESSION IN GERMANY

Nazi poster, 1931. This poster, advertising the Nazi Party, shows Germany as a man handcuffed by the Versailles Treaty. The poster suggests that the fire of the Nazi Party will help Germany break free.

The First World War (1914–18) was won by the Allies (Britain, France, Italy, United States). The Allies felt that the war was Germany's fault. At the end of the war, they wanted to humble Germany and ensure it could never fight again. Defeated Germany was forced to sign an agreement—the Versailles Treaty. This banned Germany from making weapons, reduced the German army to just a token force, and took control of some of Germany's key industrial areas.

▼ **Handout line, Hanover, 1930.** Millions of Germans faced poverty and starvation. Ordinary people grew more and more resentful as they lined up for soup or a chance at casual work.

▶**Berlin cabaret.** A poster advertising Carow's comedy in Berlin, 1930. Berlin in particular was famous for its wild cabarets and nightlife, where people went to forget their problems.

In addition, Germany was forced to pay large sums of money to the Allies in reparation (compensation) for the cost of the war. Germany rapidly became extremely poor. The economy plunged into depression and millions lost their jobs. The government printed money to pay for goods and services, but the more they printed, the less value it had. Middle-class Germans saw their life savings become worthless.

In desperation, some Germans turned to Communism; others lived a wild life without caring. Many Germans, however, looked for strong leadership and a renewed pride in Germany. Some people argued that Germany would not have lost the war if it had not been betrayed by "enemies within."

▶**Worthless money.** Here, German children use bundles of banknotes as toy bricks.

▲ **Five-million mark note, 1923.** As German inflation spiraled out of control, even a five-million mark note had almost no value.

▲ Saar valley, 1935.
Hitler ignored the Versailles Treaty and reclaimed the rich industrial Saar valley, which the treaty had given to France.

▼ Nazi rallies. The Nazis organized huge patriotic rallies, the most famous being the Nuremberg Rallies. (Below) Hitler arrives at a Nuremberg Rally. Banners display the swastika—the Nazi symbol.

HITLER'S RISE TO POWER

A man named Adolf Hitler (1889–1945) believed he could solve Germany's problems. He founded the National Socialist (Nazi) Party to put into practice his ideas of strong leadership and racial purity. He promised to rebuild Germany and create jobs.

The Nazi philosophy was based on the idea of an Aryan "master race" superior to all other races. This Aryan master race was epitomized by tall, blond, blue-eyed Germans. Groups the Nazis believed were impure included Slavs from Central and Eastern Europe, gypsies, blacks, and many others. But the Jews were said to be the main enemies of the Aryan master race, and the cause of Germany's defeat in 1918.

In the late 1920s, Hitler's Nazi Party started to win power. Their militant supporters, the SA, were known as Brownshirts because of the uniform they wore. People learned to fear these organized, semi-official thugs. The Brownshirts bullied and threatened ordinary people, but they picked on Jews in particular.

In January 1933, Hitler was elected Chancellor of Germany. He was now the country's political leader and second only to President Hindenburg. Hitler quickly began his campaign to rebuild Germany. He started by re-occupying all the areas Germany had been forced to surrender under the Versailles Treaty. Many Germans saw Hitler as a hero, standing up for German pride.

▼ **Hitler Youth, flag display.** The Nazis were determined to influence the young. Children over the age of six were encouraged to join a military-style youth movement called the Hitler Youth, in which they were taught to believe in Adolf Hitler and the Nazi Party.

Racial caricatures. Cartoons from a children's book, published in 1936, show the Nazi views of the Aryan German versus the Jew.

THE NAZI REGIME

Three months after Hitler was elected Chancellor in 1933, many of his political enemies were rounded up and taken to the new concentration camp at Dachau, near Munich. This was a prison able to hold very large numbers of inmates. Soon people became afraid to criticize Hitler. But on the whole, most Germans saw nothing to criticize—they supported the way Hitler was running the country.

When President Hindenburg died in 1934, Hitler declared himself Führer, sole leader of Germany. To strengthen his control, Hitler encouraged his supporters to report to the Gestapo—the Nazi secret police—anyone they thought might be against him.

The Nazi Party worked hard to persuade people that it was patriotic to hate all "enemies of the state." Goebbels, the Nazi Minister of Propaganda, used very modern methods to persuade Germans that certain groups were their enemies, in particular the Jews.

Hitler provided jobs for people by building motorways, ships, planes, and military equipment. This was in clear violation of the Versailles Treaty. He seemed to be preparing for war. Hitler made wild speeches about getting rid of the Jews, building a bigger German "homeland," and creating a new powerful German state—the Third Reich. Most people did not take him seriously.

▼ **Work squad, 1933.** Formerly unemployed workers on their way to build a new motorway (autobahn) near Frankfurt am Main. Giving people jobs was a priority for the Nazi government.

▲ Opening ceremony at Dachau, 1933.
The Nazis held a press conference when they opened Dachau concentration camp. They wanted to show how they would deal efficiently and firmly with their enemies. The first prisoners were mostly socialists and trade unionists. More concentration camps would soon be built.

▼ Anti-Semitism for children. Children in German schools were taught to hate Jews. This Nazi schoolbook of 1936 encouraged them to tease and bully Jewish pupils and teachers.

▲ Hitler visiting a German shipyard, 1934.
Hitler ignored the Versailles Treaty, which prohibited German military development, and started to build ships, planes, and weapons.

▲ A new autobahn, 1934. Thousands were given employment building a network of wide, straight roads across Germany. When war came, these would enable Hitler's armies to travel swiftly.

KRISTALLNACHT

In 1935, Hitler made anti-Semitism official by passing the Nuremberg Laws. These deprived the Jews of their German citizenship and placed special restrictions on them. Jews were forbidden to marry non-Jews or to have non-Jewish servants. Professional associations, like those for German doctors and lawyers, expelled their Jewish members, and some schools expelled their Jewish pupils.

Such practices were imitated across Central Europe. In Poland there were anti-Jewish riots, and anti-Jewish laws were imposed in Hungary and Austria.

Besides the new laws, Jews were humiliated in the streets and picked on in schools. Soon, Jews had to carry passports with "J" stamped on them. All Jewish property had to be registered, and valuables handed over to the German authorities.

Things came to a head on November 9, 1938, when anti-Jewish riots were organized across Germany. This episode has become known as Kristallnacht (Night of [broken] glass). After these riots, more than 20,000 Jews were taken to the various new concentration camps that had been built.

Before Kristallnacht, many Jews in Germany believed that Nazi anti-Semitism was a passing phase. Afterward, most Jews were persuaded that things would only get worse. Many emigrated to other parts of Europe and to the United States.

Smashed windows in Berlin after Kristallnacht, 1938. On Kristallnacht, every Jewish shop in Berlin and other major German cities was wrecked and looted by organized gangs.

▼ Jewish lawyer, 1933. This Munich lawyer had complained about police behavior, and, so was made to parade barefoot through the streets proclaiming he would never complain again.

▲ Jews in Vienna, 1938.
These Jews were made to scrub the streets in Vienna, Austria, while the crowd looked on.

▼ A synagogue burns during Kristallnacht. Across Germany, 195 synagogues were destroyed during Kristallnacht.

BLITZKRIEG AND WAR

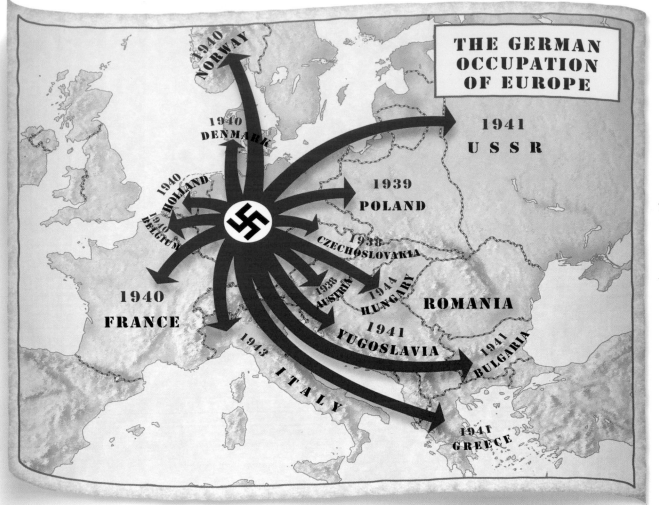

THE GERMAN OCCUPATION OF EUROPE

1940 NORWAY

1940 DENMARK

1940 HOLLAND

1940 BELGIUM

1939 POLAND

1941 USSR

1938 CZECHOSLOVAKIA

1938 AUSTRIA

1944 HUNGARY

ROMANIA

1940 FRANCE

1941 YUGOSLAVIA

1941 BULGARIA

1943 ITALY

1941 GREECE

While Hitler had been strengthening his control within Germany, he had also been strengthening Germany's position within Europe. He had reclaimed parts of Germany in 1935; in 1938 he had annexed Austria and part of Czechoslovakia; in 1939 he invaded the rest of Czechoslovakia. World leaders, desperate to avoid another war, had hoped that by allowing him to do this, he would be satisfied.

But when Germany invaded Poland in September 1939, Britain and France finally realized that Hitler would have to be stopped. They declared war. However, by now, Hitler had built up a powerful and efficient German army. Within weeks, his policy of Blitzkrieg (lightning war)—attacking quickly and strongly—had enabled him to sweep across Poland.

The following year, it again took only a few weeks for the German armies to spread westward across Norway, Belgium, Holland, and France. Millions of Jews who had thought they were safe from the Nazis suddenly found themselves under German rule and unable to escape.

▲ Stuka dive-bombers, 1939. Aerial attacks were a vital aspect of Blitzkrieg, allowing the Germans to wipe out opposition behind the enemy lines.

▶ Invading Poland, 1939. The mechanized army units that Hitler had built up over the past six years enabled him to sweep across Poland, destroying villages in his way, before any resistance could be organized.

▼ Germans in Paris, 1940. Outmaneuvering the French defenses, by advancing through Belgium and Holland, Hitler's forces entered Paris within months of the start of his western campaign.

"ENEMIES OF THE STATE"

▲ **Blood tests for gypsies.** A doctor takes blood from a gypsy woman. The Nazis taught, wrongly, that you could identify gypsies by their blood. Hundreds of thousands of gypsies were murdered during the Holocaust.

The Nazis swiftly enforced the Nuremberg Laws against the Jews throughout their newly occupied territories. At the same time, they continued to tighten their control over the Jews in Germany and Austria.

Mock-scientific evidence was developed to support their theory that gypsies, blacks, Slavs, and especially Jews were racially inferior. Erroneous tests were devised to determine these "inferior" races. Once racial type had been established, everything was done to ensure that these groups were kept separate from the "pure-blooded" Aryans.

Having learned to live with the Nuremberg Laws, Jews now had to

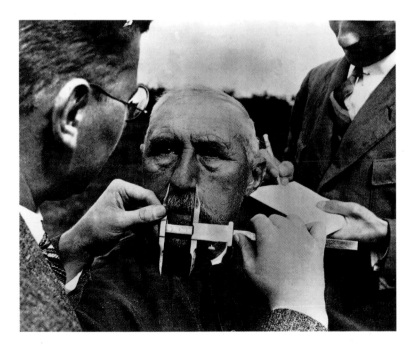

▲ **Measuring noses.** Nazis believed that you could recognize Jews by the shape of their noses. This led to many people, both Jews and non-Jews, being intimidated because their noses were a certain shape.

wear yellow stars and armbands to show their "racial" type. There were also strict laws enforced to prevent any non-Jews from mixing with Jews. These new laws meant that, across Europe, Jews started to be separated from the rest of the population.

In nearly every country they invaded, the Nazis found local people who were only too willing to help them identify and condemn their Jewish neighbors.

▼ **Political prisoners.** Communists, trade unionists, and liberals were also considered enemies of the state and were watched and labeled accordingly. Here, political prisoners are being registered at a Nazi concentration camp.

Labeling Jews. New laws were introduced to separate Jews from their non-Jewish neighbors. Every Jew had to carry an identity card (above). Soon they had to wear yellow stars (left) or armbands (below) as well.

◄ Harassment. Interrogation by German soldiers was a daily feature of life in the ghettoes. Depending on the answers they gave, many civilians were either shot or sent to concentration camps.

◄ Starvation. A child dying of starvation on the streets of the Warsaw ghetto in Poland. Thousands of Jews died in the terrible conditions.

"I was forced into the Lodz ghetto in Poland in May 1940. Eight of us shared a small room. German sentries round the outside of the ghetto perimeter shot dead Jews who ventured too near the barbed wire fencing. People were regularly deported to the 'work camps', never to be heard of again. I became a postman, which entitled me to a double ration of soup. Basic food rations were distributed once a fortnight, so starving people ate theirs quickly and then had nothing else to eat for days. In the spring of 1941, my mother died of starvation.

Michael
A Holocaust survivor

GHETTOES

Most European cities at this time had areas where Jews had settled over the years. Often these areas were in the poorer part of a town. Under the Nazis, all Jews from a city and its environs were now herded into these areas, called ghettoes. Walls were built around the ghettoes and Nazi guards were posted at the gates to make sure that no Jews escaped. No one was allowed to leave the ghettoes without a special permit.

Conditions inside the ghettoes were very harsh: extreme poverty, terrible overcrowding, and little sanitation. Many thousands died of starvation and disease. Jews on the ghetto streets were routinely humiliated by soldiers and guards. Those who were strong enough were taken away to work as slave laborers for the Nazis.

The hundreds of thousands of Jews, crammed into these ghettoes from all the surrounding areas, tried to keep life going as before. Many ran schools, held concerts, produced newspapers, and organized medical care.

▼ **Street scene, Warsaw ghetto.** There were so many people living in the ghetto that the streets were always crowded. Here, all the Jews are wearing armbands—even the policeman—and the streetcar is marked with a Star of David.

21

DEATH SQUADS

◄ **Poland, 1940.** A Jewish man is forced to pray in public before being shot. Often Jews were massacred in broad daylight. Not content with killing, the occupying forces also mocked and humiliated their victims, while local people looked on.

The German occupation of Eastern Europe gave the Nazis control over millions of Jews. Many of these Jews were poor and had not been particularly well integrated into non-Jewish society. This made them more vulnerable than the German Jews of the 1930s. It was here, in Eastern Europe, that the Nazis began the genocide—their large-scale and systematic campaign to destroy all Jews.

Special army units, called Einsatzgruppen, were set up by the SS, the elite Nazi force. At first, they inflicted small-scale humiliations and massacres on the Jews in Central Europe. But when Germany invaded the USSR in 1941, the Einsatzgruppen started an organized, sweeping massacre of Jews, from Poland across all the occupied areas of the USSR.

Going from village to village and ghetto to ghetto, the Einsatzgruppen rounded up all Jews. Those who might be useful as slave labor were sent to the concentration camps. There they would soon be worked to death. The remainder—the women, the children, the elderly, the sick—were herded together by the Einsatzgruppen, taken into the countryside, and shot. In many places, the Nazis found willing local people to carry out this task.

◄ **Forced labor, Poland, c.1943.** Able-bodied Jews were used for slave labor

▶ **Jew at a mass grave, Ukraine.** Across Eastern Europe, Jews were killed just outside the towns their families had lived in for hundreds of years.

▼ **Women being led into the woods.** In many places Jewish women and children were taken away by Einsatzgruppen to be executed.

CONCENTRATION CAMPS

The first Nazi concentration camps were in Germany. Later, other camps were built in the occupied territories of Eastern Europe. Away from the public eye, prisoners there were treated even more harshly than in the German camps.

The camps contained a cross section of those considered undesirable by the Nazis: large numbers of Jews, but also political prisoners, journalists, trade unionists, gypsies, homosexuals, and Jehovah's Witnesses, among others. We know this because the Nazis kept meticulous records, detailing not only each prisoner's name, number, and date of arrival, but also the reason for their detention, any offenses committed, punishments given, and eventually, usually, the cause and date of death.

Once at the camps, instead of names, the prisoners were given numbers, which were tattooed onto their wrists. Punishments were savage and prisoners could be shot for the slightest offense. Food was limited, the winters were harsh, and diseases raged in the overcrowded conditions. Prisoners slept in huge dormitories with up to ten prisoners sharing a bed. Many prisoners were used like laboratory animals for medical experiments. Others were taken as slave laborers to factories and quarries nearby.

▶ **Auschwitz, Poland, today.** The concentration camp has been left as it was as a memorial to those who died there.

◀ **New arrivals.** These teenage prisoners at Auschwitz were photographed for the records. When people arrived at the camps, their clothes were taken from them, their heads were shaved, and they were tattooed with a number.

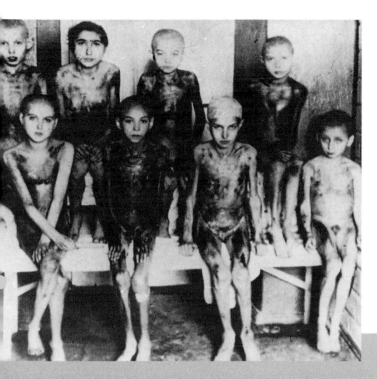

◄ **Medical research.** Nazi doctors used prisoners, like these girls at Auschwitz, as human guinea pigs, and conducted painful experiments on them. Without anesthetics or aftercare, many died from such cruel treatment.

▲ **Prisoner's possessions.** A plate, cup, spoon, and fork from Majdanek camp in Czechoslovakia.

❝ *The tattooing was not a pleasant experience, especially if you bear in mind how primitive the tool was with which it was carried out. Of course it hurt. There was blood and a nasty swelling afterwards. The shaving off of our hair was the most traumatic experience. It made me feel utterly vulnerable and reduced to a complete nobody. I had relinquished my clothes as well, and I stood there stark naked, bald and with a number on my arm. In the space of a few minutes I had been stripped of every vestige of human dignity and become indistinguishable from everyone around me.* **❞**

Anita
A Holocaust survivor

"THE FINAL SOLUTION"

By 1941, Nazi leaders realized that there were so many Jews in occupied Europe that, with existing methods, it would take a long time to eliminate them all. Though about two million Jews had already been killed by the Einsatzgruppen, there were still ghettoes and camps full of Jews all over Europe. In January 1942, at the Wannsee Conference, the Nazi leadership decided on "The Final Solution to the Jewish Problem."

This "Final Solution" involved using modern factory methods to "process" Jews to death in the fastest possible time. To do this, some of the concentration camps in the east were converted into "death camps". They were equipped with poison gas chambers, disguised as showers, and crematoria with rows of ovens. From the ghettoes, Jews would be transferred by train to the death camps. On arrival, some prisoners would be selected for slave labor. The rest would be led to the "showers" and gassed. The bodies would be burnt in the crematoria.

Unaware of what awaited them, many Jews were happy to leave the misery of the ghettoes to go to the camps. Even when they were walking naked into the gas chambers, most did not realize what was really happening.

▲ **Boarding the train at Lublin.**
Jews were transported to the camps in cattle-trucks. Without adequate food or water, many died on the way.

▼ Sorting the belongings. Jews going to the death camps were told to take a suitcase with them. At the camp, the belongings of those sent to the gas chambers were sorted for use by the Nazis and their local helpers.

▲ Sorting the prisoners. New arrivals at Auschwitz waiting in lines of men and women. Camp officials immediately separated new arrivals into those who might work for a while and those who would be killed right away.

ACTIVE RESISTANCE

Throughout the war, both Jews and non-Jews in occupied Europe resisted the Nazis. These resistance fighters were known as partisans. They secretly collected weapons, blew up railway lines, and ambushed Nazis in the woods. Across Europe, many Jews escaped from the ghettoes and the concentration camps to join the partisans.

The Jewish resistance to the Nazis increased as more people were deported and as rumors of the death camps began to reach the ghettoes. Several ghettoes organized revolts. At Bialystock in Poland, 40,000 Jews died defending the ghetto against deportations. But the most famous revolt was the Warsaw ghetto uprising.

In April 1943, German troops surrounded the Warsaw ghetto with the intention of rounding up all remaining Jews, but the Jews fought back. The two sides were not evenly matched but, by moving around and through the network of sewers, the Jews managed to hold back the German advance for several weeks. However, by May, the ghetto was reduced to rubble.

There were occasional revolts in the death camps, too. During a revolt at Sobibor death camp, many guards were killed and more than 600 Jewish prisoners managed to escape and join local partisans.

▶ **Jewish partisans.** Jewish partisans wait in the woods to ambush German troops.

▶ **The end of the Warsaw ghetto uprising.** On April 19, 1943, the Jews in the Warsaw ghetto rose up against the Nazis. The revolt was crushed three weeks later, the ghetto destroyed, and the few survivors transported to the death camps.

HELPERS

Large numbers of people, both Jews and non-Jews, risked their lives to save people from the Nazis. By doing so, they showed that it was possible to defy the Nazi regime. They also inspired people around them to see that there were basic principles and ideas concerning human rights and responsibilities that they were not prepared to give up.

Miep Gies

Miep Gies was a young secretary in Amsterdam, Holland. After the German invasion of Holland in May 1940, severe anti-Semitic laws were soon imposed. Otto Frank, Gies's Jewish boss, arranged for his family to go into hiding in a secret attic above the offices. Generously, he shared this cramped space with another family. Their only source of food and daily news was from Gies and a couple of other close friends. Gies risked her life every day for nearly two years until they were betrayed. The two families were sent to the camps, where seven out of eight of them died. After they had gone, Gies found Frank's daughter's diary in the empty attic. When Frank, the only survivor, returned after the war, she gave it to him. *The Diary of Anne Frank* is now world famous.

Janusz Korzcak

Janusz Korzcak was a Polish-Jewish doctor and educator who had become famous before the war. His best-known book is called *How to Love Children*. He founded an orphanage in Warsaw, Poland. On August 12, 1942, the order came for the children from his orphanage to be deported to the camps. Korzcak was told that he did not have to go, because doctors were still needed in Warsaw's ghetto. However, Korzcak refused to leave "his" children, knowing how scared they would be without him. With great dignity, he led the children in a well-ordered procession into the cattle-trucks destined for the camp at Treblinka. The children did not cry, because the doctor was with them. None of them was ever seen alive again.

King Christian X of Denmark

Despite the fact that Denmark was occupied by the Germans from 1940 onward, King Christian and his government refused to enact Nazi-style anti-Semitic laws. For example, they would not allow the yellow star to be introduced. Eventually the Nazis became impatient and decided to round up the Jews themselves. But German officials leaked the plan to Danish politicians, who warned the Jews. Nearly every Jew was smuggled to safety in neutral Sweden. However, 464 Jews were captured and taken to Theresienstadt concentration camp in Czechoslovakia. Even then, the king did not forget his Jewish subjects but constantly urged the Germans to provide them with food and medicine, and not kill them. Eventually, Danish officials were allowed to visit them. One visitor whispered to a Jewish prisoner: "I deliver the King's most sincere regards. He is always thinking of you." Danish Jews knew they were not forgotten.

Raoul Wallenberg

Raoul Wallenberg was a Swedish diplomat who arrived in Budapest, Hungary, in June 1944. Hitler was desperately accelerating the extermination of the Jews. Wallenberg's job was to protect Hungarian Jews who had ties with Sweden. But, he went further. He invented his own documents with official-looking stamps and crests and gave them to whomever he could. He established hospitals and soup kitchens and employed Jews in them. He moved Jews into blocks of apartments over which he flew the Swedish flag. He intercepted Jews being transported to the death camps and gave them protective passports. Besides saving over 100,000 Jews himself, he also inspired the neutral Swiss and Spanish to start imitating him. Sadly, when the Russians liberated Budapest, they thought he might be a spy. He was arrested and never seen again.

TIME RUNS OUT

In June 1942, the BBC broadcast the first news of the mass destruction of Jews; finally the rest of the world learned about the atrocities taking place in Europe. In November, the Allies announced that those responsible would be punished. In June 1943, Heinrich Himmler, the head of the SS, organized slave-labor units to dig up and burn corpses to destroy the evidence.

From 1943 on, as the Nazis realized they were losing the war, they accelerated the slaughter of Jews. Whole ghettoes were wiped out. Deportations to the death camps were speeded up until even the most efficient camps, like Auschwitz, could not cope with the numbers they had to kill each day. Countries like Denmark and Hungary, which had resisted deporting their Jews, were put under increasing pressure to do so.

It was now a race against time. As advancing Soviet armies forced the Germans to retreat from Eastern Europe, starving and weak camp inmates were marched across Europe from camp to camp in what became known as the Death Marches. At the same time, resistance strengthened, both among Jews and in some occupied countries that feared being accused of helping with the slaughter.

▲ **Round up in Hungary, 1944.** As defeat came closer, the Nazis began to concentrate on countries from which few Jews had been taken so far, like Hungary. Hundreds of thousands were deported and killed in the final months of the war.

> **"** *After the Russians encircled Budapest on 25th December 1944, the Nazis intensified the killing. Within days, I was taken, with 280 other men, women, and children, stripped naked in the freezing Hungarian midwinter and marched to the Danube river. After lining us up, machine-gunners mowed us down into the icy water. With nothing more to lose, I jumped before I was shot. I stayed underwater and drifted downstream. When I could hardly feel my limbs any longer, I climbed out and crawled back to the terrible conditions in the ghetto. I was the only member of my extended family of 27 members to survive.* **"**

John
A Holocaust survivor

▲ **Bodies on a wood pyre, 1945.** Toward the end of the war, the crematoria in the death camps simply could not cope with the huge number of bodies to be burned. Makeshift alternative arrangements were made.

▼ **Prisoner records.** The Nazis had kept detailed records of their massacre of the Jews. At the end of the war, they tried to destroy this evidence, but many records were discovered still in the camps.

◄ **Bodies found at Buchenwald, Germany.** Despite desperate attempts by the Nazis to destroy the evidence of what they had done, Allied armies arrived at the camps too quickly for all the dead to have been disposed of.

LIBERATING THE CAMPS

As Allied forces closed in on Nazi Germany from both east and west, they began to discover the concentration camps and death camps. Despite the rumors, and reports from the few who had escaped, nothing had prepared the world for what they found. There had been concentration camps before, but never had there been these death camps where so many millions could be killed so ruthlessly and efficiently.

As camp officials fled before the advancing armies, huge numbers of dead and dying were left abandoned. Many camps had been staffed by local militia. Most of these men and women quickly deserted to their homes and disappeared.

Those guards who were caught were pressed into service by the shocked Allied troops, at least to bury the bodies. Some of the liberated inmates died after liberation, sometimes because their starved bodies could not cope with the improved nutrition they now received; or because they at last relaxed their efforts to stay alive and bear witness; or else because diseases like typhoid continued to rage through the camps.

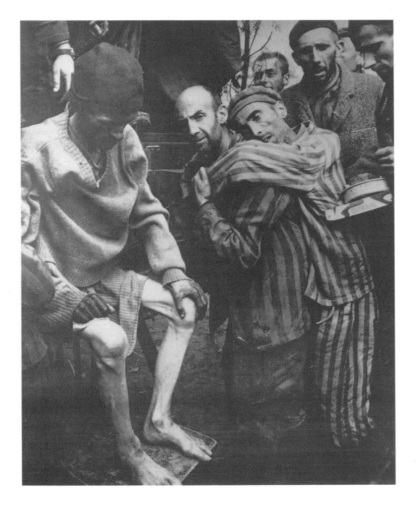

▲ **Survivors, Wöbbelin, Germany.** As at other camps, survivors at Wöbbelin were in desperate need of medical care. The terrible condition of the survivors deeply shocked the Allied soldiers who liberated the camps.

▲ Survivors at Buchenwald. As the Holocaust drew to a close, slave laborers were crammed into ever more crowded conditions. These survivors from Buchenwald were among the lucky few to be found alive.

▶ SS guards forced to bury the dead. Many bodies remained unburied after the camps were liberated. Here female SS guards at Bergen-Belsen camp in Germany are made to bury the people they helped to kill.

◀ Looking for glasses, Wöbbelin. A survivor at Wöbbelin picks through a pile of glasses that had once belonged to fellow prisoners, hoping to find a pair suitable for him—or even his own.

THE SURVIVORS

◄ **Child survivors of Auschwitz.** Thousands of orphans were found when the camps were liberated. Many had been used as human guinea pigs in medical experiments. More than 1.5 million Jewish children were killed in the Holocaust.

▲ **Displaced persons, 1945.** For many, the journey home was long and hard. These Jews are returning on foot to their homes in Poland. Many of those returning met with a very hostile reception.

For many camp inmates and other survivors, the ordeal did not stop even after liberation. Criss-crossing Europe, these "displaced persons," as they were called, often found they had no home and no family left. "Displaced Persons Camps" were established for them.

Those who did get back to their former homes sometimes found other people living in them. Often, the new inhabitants were not willing to give up the home, and resented the return of the original owner.

"Displaced persons" who could not return home had to find a country willing to accept them as citizens.

Thousands of Jews hoped to settle in Israel—the historical Jewish homeland. However, the British refused most Jews entry to Israel (which was then under British control) for fear that the arrival of too many Jews at once would upset the tense balance there between Jews and Arabs. Jews caught by the British trying to enter Israel were imprisoned on the island of Cyprus.

In time though, most survivors established new lives wherever they could, and began the attempt to forget their hellish experiences.

▼ **A camp survivor identifying a guard.**
For many prisoners, identifying those guards who were particularly cruel was a step on the road to honoring the dead.

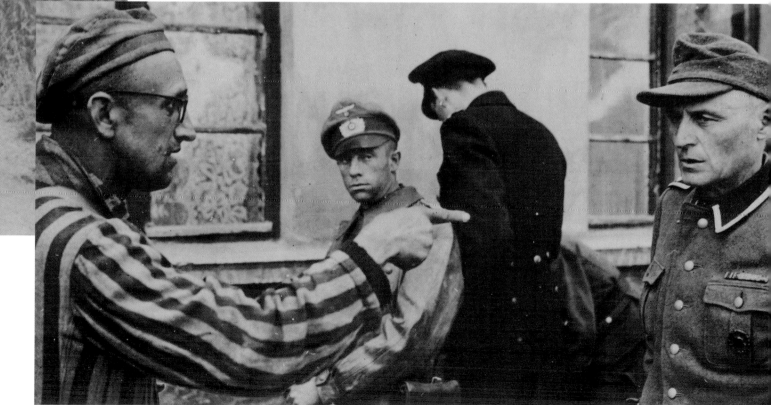

TRUTH AND JUSTICE

In 1945 in Nuremberg, where the Nazi racial laws had been announced ten years earlier, 22 leaders of the Nazi regime were put on trial: for breaking the rules of war and for crimes against humanity. Of them, 19 defendants were found guilty, mostly condemned by the evidence they themselves had efficiently compiled.

However, it did not end there. Even today, Nazi war criminals are still being found who have been in hiding all that time. Occasionally they are put on trial, though many of the witnesses to their crimes are now very old.

New issues of justice are constantly coming to light. Valuables that were stolen or confiscated from Holocaust victims have not been returned. In some cases, insurance companies have not paid claims because survivors cannot supply death certificates for those killed in the camps.

To begin with, most survivors just wanted to try to forget what had happened to them and get on with their lives. Now they are aging, however, often living alone with their memories, sometimes in poverty, and thoughts of what they lost have come flooding back.

▶ **Townspeople burying the dead, 1945.** Local citizens living near the camps were made to take some responsibility for clearing up the horror that had happened in their neighborhood. Many said they had not known what went on in the camps.

Germans visiting Buchenwald. In many areas, German civilians were forced to walk through camp crematoria to see what their Nazi rulers had been doing.▼

Nuremberg Trials, 1945. While several of the leading Nazis escaped justice by committing suicide (like Hitler, Himmler, and Goebbels) or fleeing the country (like Eichmann), several others were found guilty at Nuremberg and executed.

Simon Wiesenthal. Wiesenthal, a survivor of ▲ the Holocaust, has worked tirelessly to identify Nazi criminals who fled the country or changed their identities. Over the years, he has brought over 1,000 Nazis, including Eichmann, to justice.

COULD IT HAPPEN AGAIN?

At the Nuremberg Trials, crimes against humanity were for the first time defined as a punishable offense. However, calling something a crime does not prevent people from doing it.

Modern communications technology means that, in theory, it should be impossible for anyone ever again to kill so many millions without the world knowing about it. But between 1975 and 1979 more than a million people were killed in Cambodia, even though technology meant that news of the massacres reached the outside world. Just as during the Holocaust, eyewitness accounts were not taken seriously for a long time. This reminds us that people have to *look* if they want to see.

In Rwanda in 1994, there were international peacekeepers and aid workers all around as Hutus massacred Tutsis. There was no doubt about what was happening, but nobody could decide if it was any of their business to stop the bloodshed.

In the 1990s, in the former Yugoslavia, the Serbs tried to create a racially pure Serbian homeland, by driving out other ethnic groups such as Muslims. This led to terrible massacres in Bosnia and, later, Kosovo. Although deploring the situation, the international community for a long time stood by, endlessly uncertain about whether it could intervene in what was viewed as a local conflict.

▶ **Cambodia, 1979.** The appalling scale of destruction by the Cambodian dictator Pol Pot was not discovered for some time. But even the evidence of the "killing fields" left many people in the West feeling it was happening too far away to be their concern.

▼▶ Rwanda, 1994. When the resentment between the Hutus and the Tutsis in Rwanda finally boiled over, it took the international community crucial months to decide what to do. By the time it intervened, millions were homeless and one million were dead.

▼ Concentration camp in Bosnia, 1992. Photographs of Croats and Muslims in a Serbian camp shocked many people, but the international community still reacted slowly.

THE LESSONS OF HISTORY

When the Nazi camps were liberated at the end of the Second World War, many people felt something must be done to stop anything like the Holocaust from happening again. In 1948 the United Nations published the Universal Declaration of Human Rights, which had been written in reaction to the Holocaust. It has since been adopted by every country in the United Nations.

The idea of "universal human rights," which apply equally to all people, was quite new. The Declaration gives a universal standard for all governments to aspire to. While this does not stop tyrants and dictators, it means that there are clear rules that they can be seen to have transgressed and by which they can then be judged.

Now therefore The General Assembly proclaims this
UNIVERSAL DECLARATION of HUMAN RIGHTS
as a common standard of achievement for all peoples and all nations

1   Right to equality
2   Freedom from discrimination
3   Right to life, liberty, personal security
4   Freedom from slavery
5   Freedom from torture, degrading treatment
6   Right to recognition as a person before the law
7   Right to equality before the law
8   Right to remedy by competent tribunal
9   Freedom from arbitrary arrest or exile
10   Right to fair public hearing
11   Right to be considered innocent until proven guilty
12   Freedom from interference with privacy, family, home & correspondence
13   Right to free movement in and out of the country
14   Right to asylum in other countries from persecution
15   Right to a nationality and freedom to change it
16   Right to marriage and family
17   Right to own property
18   Freedom of belief and religion
19   Freedom of opinion and information
20   Right of peaceful assembly and association
21   Right to participate in Government and in free elections
22   Right to social security
23   Right to desirable work and to join Trade Unions
24   Right to rest and leisure
25   Right to an adequate living standard
26   Right to education
27   Right to participate in the cultural life of the community
28   Right to social order assuring Human Rights

IMPORTANT DATES

1918
Nov Germany is defeated in the First World War. Germany is forced to pay huge amounts to the victorious Allies, give up areas to Poland, Lithuania, and France, reduce its army to virtually nothing, and give up control of the Rhineland industrial area.

1919
Jun The humiliating Versailles Treaty is very reluctantly signed by the defeated Germans. The British prime minister predicts that the terms are so savage that they will have to fight another war in 25 years.
Jul Germany is declared a democratic republic. But because of the very difficult social and economic conditions, the constitution allows for a president with far-reaching powers in an emergency.

1922
Aug Value of the German mark starts to collapse.

1923
Jan France sends troops into Germany to try to force it to hand over the goods and money it owes under the Versailles Treaty. German workers refuse to cooperate, and there are many strikes and much sabotage. Nazi Party holds its first rally in Munich.
Jun German mark is now 622,000 to the British pound. (At the end of the First World War, it was worth 43.3 marks to the pound.)
Nov Hitler's first attempt at revolution ends in failure and he is jailed. The mark is now worth 20 *trillion* to the pound.

1924
Apr Hitler is found guilty of treason, but is offered parole after six months.

1925
Jul Hitler publishes *Mein Kampf* (*My Struggle*). It is clear from the book what he believes and how he intends to destroy the Jews.

1927
Jul Workers' riots crushed in Vienna. Many people are shocked by the growing power of the Communists.

1929
May Extensive workers' riots in Berlin as the economy crashes.

1930
Sep In a surprise result, the Nazis come second in the German general election. The appalling economic conditions in Germany have led more people to vote for the extremes of Nazism and Communism.

1932
Apr Germany's President Hindenburg only narrowly regains his presidency against a challenge from Hitler, who has increased his share of the vote with a brilliant election campaign, masterminded by Goebbels and funded by frustrated German industrialists who want a firm government to control Communist workers.
Jul In another election, Nazis become the biggest party in the German government.
Aug German's Chancellor Von Papen and President Hindenburg refuse to give any government posts to the Nazis because of the street violence of their supporters, the Brownshirts.
Nov In another election, the Nazis lose many seats, but remain the largest party.

1933
Jan After an increase in street violence between Nazis and Communists, Von Papen and Hindenburg agree to Hitler becoming chancellor in the hope that he can tame his gangs.
Feb A mysterious fire in the Reichstag, Germany's Parliament, is blamed on the Communists, and Hitler persuades President Hindenburg to give him sweeping powers "to protect the State."
Mar Concentration camp at Dachau is opened. Hitler secures full powers from Parliament after extensive intimidation of his opponents.
Apr Nazi-inspired boycott of Jewish-owned shops. Many Jewish professionals are prevented from entering their offices.
May Hitler replaces law courts and judges with his own legal system.
Jun Hitler bans all opposition parties.
Jul Nazis issue decrees requiring the sterilization of anyone with physical or mental disabilities in an attempt to ensure that all Germans born thereafter will be perfect.
Aug President Hindenburg dies. Hitler immediately declares himself Führer.

1935
Mar Hitler takes back the industrial Saar valley. The Allies allow it, hoping that this will satisfy Hitler, even though he also introduces conscription and starts a rearmament program.
Sep Nuremberg Laws are passed, defining Jews as non-Aryans. Jews lose their pensions and are banned from teaching, farming, and the media. Jews are prohibited from employing non-Jewish staff.
Nov Further laws strip Jews of their citizenship and remove Jews from civil service and state-paid jobs.

1936
Mar Hitler occupies the Rhineland. The Allies hold back again. Anti-Jewish riots take place in Poland.

1938
Mar Hitler enters Austria, cheered by huge crowds. Four days later, anti-Jewish laws are imposed in Austria.
Apr Process of registering and confiscating Jewish property in Germany starts.
May Anti-Jewish laws are imposed in Hungary.
Jul German professional organizations —doctors, lawyers, etc—start to expel their Jewish members.
Nov Kristallnacht—coordinated anti-

Jewish riots take place across Germany. One week later, Jewish children are expelled from German schools.

1939

Jan Hitler threatens that if war starts, he will annihilate the Jews.

Mar Germany marches into Czechoslovakia. The Allies hold back, but Britain pledges to defend Poland against any German aggression.

Sep Germany invades Poland. The Allies declare war. Four weeks later, Poland is totally occupied.

Nov Yellow star is imposed on the three million Jews of Poland.

1940

Apr Germany invades Denmark and Norway. In days they are occupied. Danish and Norwegian governments declare that Jews are protected.

May Belgium and Holland are defeated and occupied.

Jun France is defeated and divided. The North is occupied, and the South becomes Vichy France under French rule but willing to cooperate with Germany.

Oct Warsaw ghetto is established. Vichy France and Romania both introduce anti-Jewish laws.

1941

Feb Deportation of Dutch Jews begins. In protest, Dutch workers call General Strike which is savagely crushed in two days.

Apr Germany invades Yugoslavia and Greece. Croatians start anti-Jewish and anti-Serb riots in support of Nazi invaders.

Jun Germany invades USSR (Soviet Union). Einsatzgruppen start slaughtering Jews, gypsies, and USSR officials in tens of thousands.

Aug Romanians start expelling Jews. In the Ukraine, Ukrainian militia start massacring Hungarian Jewish refugees.

Sep First experiments with gas chambers at Auschwitz.

Oct All Jewish emigration from Nazi-occupied lands is banned.

Dec Jews and gypsies are killed in mobile "gas vans" disguised as ambulances.

1942

Jan Wannsee Conference—Nazi leaders agree plans for "The Final Solution." Jewish resistance groups set up in Vilna and Kovno in Lithuania.

Mar Liquidation of Polish Jewry starts. Jews from Slovakia and France are deported to Auschwitz. Bulgarian Parliament vetoes deportation of Bulgarian Jews.

Jun BBC broadcasts news of mass killing of Jews.

Jul Dutch, Belgian, and Luxembourg Jews are deported to Auschwitz. Warsaw Jews are deported to Treblinka. Warsaw Jewish Resistance is formed.

Sep About 50,000 Jews are killed or removed from the Warsaw ghetto. The ghetto is demolished, leaving a small handful of Jews behind, heavily guarded and still surrounded by walls and barbed wire. Without food or medicine, they are expected to die soon.

Oct Jews in Brest-Litovsk (USSR) are massacred by SS. Norwegian Jews are deported to Auschwitz.

Nov In Bialystock in Poland, 170,000 Jews are killed in one week. Allies publicly denounce the killings and say those responsible will be punished.

1943

Mar Greek Jews are deported to Treblinka. Ghetto in Cracow, Poland, is liquidated.

Apr Warsaw ghetto uprising starts. To the surprise of the SS, it proves extremely difficult to defeat. Lithuanian Jews are massacred.

May Warsaw ghetto uprising is finally crushed.

Jun Lvov ghetto is liquidated.

Aug A revolt in Treblinka concentration camp is crushed.

Bialystock ghetto revolt is crushed. All Bialystock Jews are wiped out.

Sep With the help of their non-Jewish neighbors, Danish Jews escape to safety in neutral Sweden. Vilna ghetto is liquidated.

Oct Successful breakout from Sobibor concentration camp. After Italy changes sides, Germany occupies Italy and starts deportation of Italian Jews.

1944

Mar Germany occupies Hungary after Hungary tries to change sides. Eichmann put in charge of the destruction of Hungarian Jews.

Jun International pressure leads Hungary to stop deportations.

Jul Soviet Union advances. Death Marches start.

Aug Lodz ghetto Jews are all deported to Auschwitz.

Oct Unsuccessful revolt in Auschwitz.

Nov SS and Hungarian Fascists restart anti-Jewish massacres and deportations of Jews in Hungary.

1945

Jan Auschwitz is liberated by the Soviet Union.

Apr Buchenwald, Bergen-Belsen, and Dachau are liberated by the Allies. Hitler commits suicide. His suicide note blames the Jews for the downfall of Germany.

May Death Marches cease. Germany surrenders. 1,000 Jews attempting to return to their homes in Poland are killed by local Poles when they arrive.

Nov Nuremberg Trials. The main leaders of Germany are tried for atrocities and crimes against humanity.

1946

Oct Nineteen Nazis are found guilty of war crimes at the Nuremberg Trials. Twelve men are condemned to death by hanging; three are sentenced to life imprisonment; four are given shorter prison sentences.

GLOSSARY

Child's jacket from Auschwitz

Anti-Semitism Hatred of Jews. A particular form of racism.

Aryan Anyone from Indo-European stock. However, the Nazis defined Aryans as only non-Jewish white people, in particular, tall people with blond hair and blue eyes.

Concentration camp A prison system for keeping large numbers of inmates using the minimum number of guards and cost. This usually results in very harsh conditions for the prisoners. The first concentration camps were devised by the British in the Boer War in South Africa (1899–1902). Some of the Nazi concentration camps were: Buchenwald, Bergen-Belsen and Dachau in Germany and Auschwitz in Poland. There are still concentration camps in some countries.

Crematorium A large oven designed to be big enough to burn dead bodies. Death camps had to install a great number of crematoria to get rid of the dead bodies.

Death camp An extermination camp. A camp designed by the Nazis to take living people in at one end and, with the least amount of trouble, kill them. To avoid revolt and panic, death camps and their gas chambers were disguised, leading people to feel that they were being taken to showers before being imprisoned. Most death camps were attached to concentration camps. The first six death camps were in

Ration card from the Lodz ghetto

Poland—Auschwitz, Chelmno, Treblinka, Sobibor, Majdanek, Belzec. At the end of the war, other concentration camps were in the process of being converted into death camps.

Death Marches As the Russian advance toward the end of the war forced the Germans to retreat, concentration camp inmates were marched out of their camps and across Europe. Those who could not keep up were shot at the roadside.

Einsatzgruppen Special squads, related to the SS, but often involving local people, whose job it was to round up Jews and massacre them nearby. They eventually gave way to the more efficient death camps.

Fascist Someone who believes in Fascism. Fascism was a very popular political attitude in the 1930s in many countries in Europe. Fascism believes in strong government by one leader. The wishes of the individual are secondary to the wishes of the state. There are still Fascist dictators in the world.

"Final Solution" The term used by the Nazis to describe the wiping out of the Jews—their "final solution" to what they saw as "the Jewish problem."

Führer Leader—the title that Hitler gave himself after the death of President Hindenburg of Germany in 1934.

Genocide Murder of a people—a word invented to describe what had been attempted by the Nazis against the Jews.

Gas chamber A Nazi invention to kill large numbers of people by poison gas. The gas chambers were rooms disguised as showers. Once the chambers were filled with people, poison gas would be poured through the shower-heads instead of water.

Gestapo The Secret Police—the most ruthless section of all the Nazi-organized groups.

Ghetto A part of a town separated by walls and gates to keep Jews apart from the rest of the town. The first ghetto was established in Venice in 1516. The Nazis established ghettoes in several major Eastern European cities. (Now the word "ghetto" is used to mean a part of town where a certain group tends to live.)

Holocaust Literally "burnt sacrifice." Now used to refer to the destruction of six million Jews and several million others in the cold-blooded attempt by the Nazis to destroy everyone that did not fit in with their racial theories about the "Master Race." The word Holocaust is sometimes used just to refer to the systematic massacre of the Jews.

Kristallnacht The Night of (Broken) Glass. The night of November 9th, 1938 when Jewish buildings all over Germany were attacked and burned.

Nazi The short form of National Socialist, the title of Hitler's party. Nazism is a particular type of Fascism which concentrates on race and racial control.

Nuremberg Laws Laws which were introduced in 1935 to define Jews as non-Aryan and therefore not German citizens.

Nuremberg Rallies Huge public rallies, giving Hitler an opportunity to inspire his followers with their monumental scale.

Child's shoes, found at Auschwitz

Nuremberg Trials Trials organized by the victorious Allies at the end of the Second World War to try the leaders of Germany for war crimes and crimes against humanity.

SA The "Storm Troops" or Brownshirts. The original Nazi force, identified by the brown shirts of their uniform. This threatening private army, numbering 400,000, gave Hitler power on the streets before he was elected in 1933.

SS The elite section of the SA. Originally formed in 1925 as a bodyguard for the party leadership, it eventually grew to 50,000 men who were distinguished by the black shirts of their uniform. They were selected for their "Aryan" looks and their commitment to Nazi teachings.

Swastika The symbol of the Nazi Party. It is a reversed form of an ancient mystic Hindu symbol.

Swastika on a Nazi armband

Third Reich "Third State." Hitler claimed that under his leadership, Germany would have a new beginning—its third—and that the Third Reich would last for a thousand years.

#

Acknowledgments

Cover photo: ©**Yad Vashem Archives, Jerusalem**
© **AFF/AFS Amsterdam, the Netherlands** p. 30l
AKG Photo, London pp. 2r, 7t, 8t, 8b, 9br, 10tr, 11l & c, 12, 13b, 17tl, 17r, 17bl, 18t, 18-19, 19br, 20b, 31l, 38c
Camera Press p. 36-37, 40-41 (Sir Russell Johnson)
Franklin Watts (with thanks to the Imperial War Museum, London) pp. 1, 19tr, 19c, 25tr, 47, 48
Hulton Getty Picture Collection pp. 5, 6b, 10l, 11r, 18bl, 21b, 33b, 35t, 38-39, 43
Mary Evans Picture Library pp. 2l, 9bl, 13tl, 13tr
Popperfoto pp. 14b, 21t, 22t, 34r, 35b, 36b (Reuters), 38l, 40t (Reuters), 41c (Reuters)
Rod Shone pp. 24-25
The Stock Market pp. 4-5
Topham Picturepoint pp. 31r, 41t (Associated Press)
Wiener Library, London/© Panstwowe Muzeum Oswiecim Brzezinka p.24
©**Yad Vashem Archives, Jerusalem** pp. 3, 10b, 13cr, 15tl, 15tr, 15b, 20t, 22c, 22-23, 25tl, 26b, 26-27, 27b, 28-29, 29b, 30r, 32-33, 33t, 34l, 37b, 39

Maps pp. 7, 16 by Julian Baker

Quotation p.25 from *Inherit the Truth 1939–1945* by Anita Lasker-Wallfisch p.71 (Giles de la Mare Publishers Limited, London, 1996).

Other quotations as told to the author.

Designed by Paul May